This book belongs to:

....

Published in 2024 by Welbeck Editions, an imprint of
Welbeck Children's Limited, part of Hachette Children's Group,
Carmelite House, 50 Victoria Embankment, London EC4Y 0DZ.
www.welbeckpublishing.com

Senior Editor: Jenni Lazell
Art Editor: Sam James
Designer: Ceri Woods
Production: Melanie Robertson

FSC
www.fsc.org
MIX
Paper | Supporting
responsible forestry
FSC® C020056

ISBN: 978-1-80338-138-1

Printed in Heshan, China

10 9 8 7 6 5 4 3 2 1

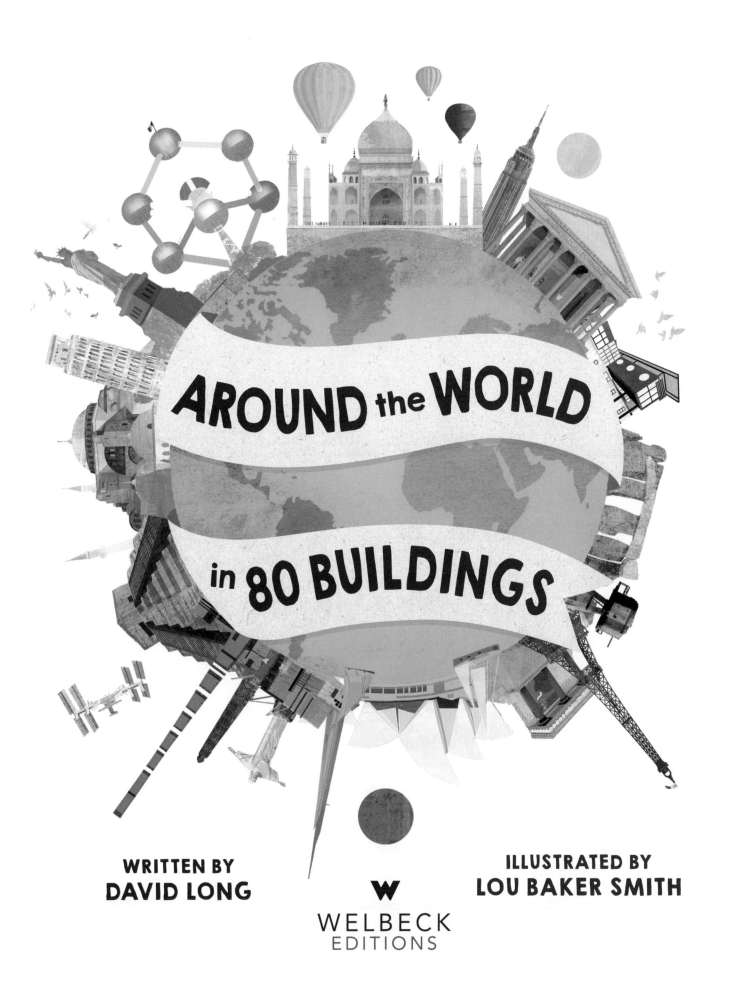

AROUND the WORLD in 80 BUILDINGS

WRITTEN BY
DAVID LONG

ILLUSTRATED BY
LOU BAKER SMITH

W

WELBECK
EDITIONS

Contents

A world of builds

The world is huge and diverse, with nearly 200 countries and many different cultures. We wear different clothes, have different customs and religions, and eat different foods. We speak more than 7,000 different languages between us but there is one thing everyone has in common. For centuries, we humans have built structures to live and work in, and to help us in our daily lives. The way these buildings look has changed dramatically over time, and so have the materials and the methods used to build them.

The first buildings

In prehistoric times, families found shelter wherever they could, often in caves that had formed naturally in cliffs and beneath rocks. Caves protected them from predators and bad weather until around 400,000 years ago when our ancestors started building shelters of their own. These first ones were simple, usually circular, huts built using whatever people found around them, such as boulders, branches, and reeds. Often the huts were built close to each other in small groups, which is how villages and then towns began to form.

Building to impress

Some of the world's most famous ancient buildings are much larger. They include the ruins of great temples, royal tombs, and richly decorated palaces, which were built by entire communities rather than individual families. Each one could take many years to complete, and buildings like these often required hundreds or even thousands of people to work on their construction. Because they were so large, and built using solid blocks of carved stone, the ruins of some of them have survived for thousands of years. By studying these carefully, historians and archaeologists can learn a lot about ancient civilizations.

Moving from A to B

For most of history people rarely traveled very far from home, but today many of the largest and most expensive modern structures are ones that make it possible for us to travel long distances by road or railroad. Deep tunnels burrow through mountains and under the sea, and in some parts of the world there are bridges that are long enough to link one country to another.

Harvesting energy

The threat of climate change has caused all sorts of new structures to be built in many countries of the world. These are ones designed to generate power sustainably, making electricity without burning fossil fuels or producing harmful emissions. The largest of these include gigantic wind farms constructed on land and out at sea, as well as vast areas of ground covered in solar panels to soak up energy from the sun.

Vanished civilizations

When an ancient civilization dies out, its language and culture can be lost forever. Often all that remains from hundreds of years and millions of lives are the spectacular ruins of its buildings. These can look strange compared to modern buildings but they give us tantalizing clues about the people who built them and the way they lived their lives.

1. Jarlshof (Shetland, 2700 BCE)

This prehistoric settlement is situated by the sea on an island approximately 125 miles north of Scotland. The remains of houses dating from many different periods of history show the site was continuously occupied for more than 4,000 years. The earliest dwellings date from the Bronze Age and Iron Age, and later Viking families moved here from Scandinavia. The most recent structure is a grand seventeenth century house but this is now ruined and there is no one living at Jarlshof today.

2. Knossos (Crete, 1900 BCE)

The great palace at Knossos was built by the Minoan people and was very luxurious for its time. As well as running water, baths, and toilets (and Europe's oldest throne), it had a maze of cool underground rooms. These provided somewhere for the owners to escape from the scorching summer sun, although according to local legends they were once occupied by a mysterious beast called the Minotaur. The Minoans developed one of the first written languages and they grew rich by trading with other people living around the Mediterranean Sea. Unfortunately, their civilization began to die out 3,500 years ago, possibly due to climate change caused by a massive volcanic eruption on the nearby island of Santorini.

3. Leptis Magna
(Libya, 2nd century)

The Roman army established the ancient world's largest empire by conquering most of Europe as well as parts of Asia and Africa. The Empire lasted for more than 500 years and Emperor Septimius Severus was its first African ruler. He spent a fortune transforming his birthplace into one of Africa's most important cities, but the empire eventually grew too big to be ruled by one man. It began to break apart as invaders attacked and defeated the once unbeatable army. Today, the ruins of his city, Leptis Magna, include some of the best-preserved Roman architecture anywhere on Earth.

The city contains an incredibly well-preserved ancient Roman theater.

4. The Kingdom of Aksum
(Ethiopia, 1st–7th centuries)

The Aksumites traded with other great empires such as Egypt, Rome, and India, which wanted the Africans' ivory, gold, rhinoceros horns, and polished tortoiseshell and paid for them using fine silks and rare spices. Many Aksumites were skilled stone masons and carved highly elaborate towers called *stelae*—the largest is 108 feet tall and weighs more than 176 tons, but no one knows what it was for or why it was built. The Aksumites also constructed large terraces so that farmers could grow food crops on steep hillsides.

5. Great Zimbabwe
(Zimbabwe, 11th century)

This royal city is ringed by high walls and was once home to nearly 20,000 people, known as the Shona. The name Zimbabwe is a Shona word meaning "stone houses" because these people were amazing builders. Thousands of stone blocks were expertly fitted together without any of the mortar or cement we see today. Some of the walls were 33 feet high and are still standing centuries later, even though no one has lived here or repaired them for more than 500 years.

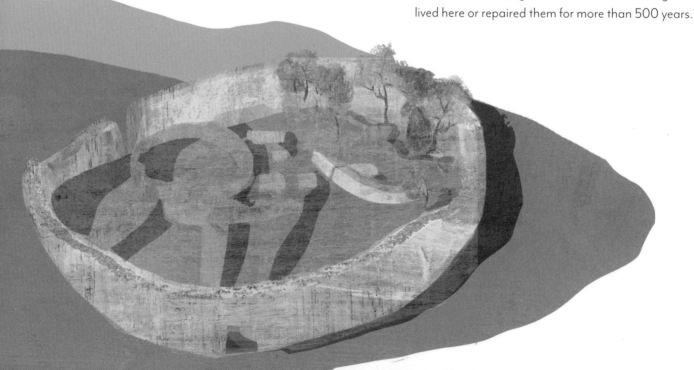

6. Angkor Wat
(Cambodia, 12th century)

Angkor Wat covers nearly 500 acres, making it the largest religious structure anywhere in the world. It was constructed for a Hindu king – but when it was attacked by an invading army, a later ruler turned it into a Buddhist temple, thinking this would protect his people. Because of this, its complex, carved stonework depicts many gods and other symbols from both religions, which is highly unusual. Many modern visitors find the temple very spooky because parts of its are covered in the winding roots and branches of trees that have grown over the site since it was abandoned in the fifteenth century.

Pyramids

Pyramids are some of the world's largest and most mysterious ancient monuments. Their appearance and purpose varies from country to country but each one is built on a perfect, square base and has four triangular sides.

7. Khufu's Pyramid (Egypt, 2600 BCE)

The oldest and most famous pyramids were built as tombs for the pharaohs who ruled Egypt for more than 3,000 years. The largest was for Pharaoh Khufu and was built using approximately 2.3 million stone blocks weighing a total of 6.6 million tons—about the same as a thousand full-grown African elephants! The building work is thought to have taken 20,000 to 30,000 workers nearly three decades. Some of the stone had to be transported by boat more than 600 miles to the site on the west bank of the River Nile and every single block then had to be cut and hauled into place by hand.

8. Pyramids of Meroë (Sudan, 3rd century BCE)

The kings and queens of neighboring Nubia also built pyramids as tombs. These rulers were less powerful than the great Egyptian pharaohs, so their tombs are much smaller, but more than 200 have survived in the deserts of what is now Sudan. Some are only 30 feet tall and unfortunately the tops of many of the larger ones were smashed off by a nineteenth century Italian explorer who came looking for treasure. The pyramids' carved stone panels and examples of Meroitic writing in some of them mean they are very interesting to archaeologists studying this ancient kingdom.

There are more pyramids in Sudan than in all of Egypt.

9. Temple of Kukulcán
(Mexico, 10th century)

The Maya, Olmec, Inca, and Aztec people built so many pyramids in Mexico and South America that ruined ones are still being discovered. Most were temples rather than tombs and, unlike the smooth sides of Egyptian pyramids, they have long flights of steps going up to a flat platform at the top. Religious ceremonies were performed at some of them by priests who climbed the steep steps to reach these platforms. Others were considered so holy that no human being was allowed to climb them or even to touch the delicately carved stonework. The most famous is the Mayan temple of Kukulcán at Chichén-Itzá, which has 91 steps running up each side. If all four sides are added up and one more added for the stone platform it makes a total of 365 steps—one for every day of the year.

10. Memphis Pyramid (USA, 1991)

The fascination with pyramids has never gone away and modern architects sometimes build them too. A famous French one forms part of the Louvre in Paris, which gets more visitors than any museum or art gallery in the world. There's an even larger one in Memphis, Tennessee, which was named after the pharaohs' ancient capital. This is a striking glass structure on the banks of the Mississippi River. It's as tall as a 32-storey building and contains a shopping mall, sports facilities, and a 100-bedroom hotel.

Tools and technology

The equipment used in construction has changed as much over the centuries as the structures themselves. The very first tools were simple ones made of stone or bone. The technology used to build modern buildings is much more sophisticated, although many of the tools are based on inventions that are much older than you might think.

Drill

Archaeologists digging at a site called Mehrgarh in what is now Pakistan have found evidence that people were using hand-operated tools called bow-drills nearly 9,000 years ago. One of their discoveries was a sharp tip made of an extremely hard stone called green jasper. This could drill holes in solid rock and even through human teeth.

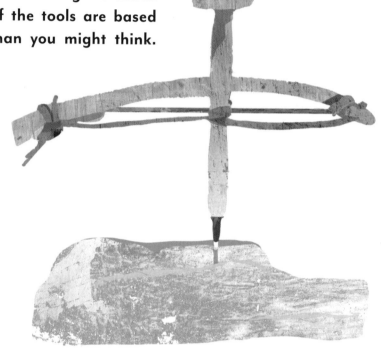

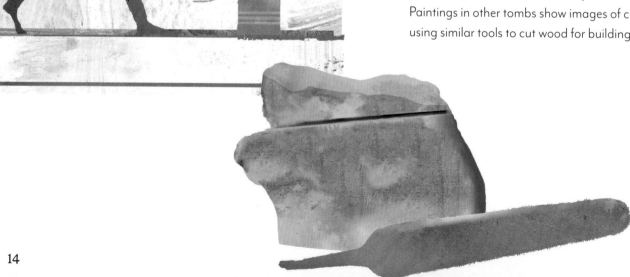

Metal saw

When pharaohs and other rich Egyptians died, they were buried with all the food, clothing, and other things their families thought they would need in the afterlife. One five-thousand-year-old tomb contained several razor-sharp saw blades made of polished copper. Paintings in other tombs show images of carpenters using similar tools to cut wood for building.

Pulleys

The Greek mathematician, astronomer, and engineer, Archimedes, described a complicated pulley system in the third century BCE, although the invention could be at least a thousand years older than this. Wooden pulleys and ropes make it possible for a person to lift much heavier weights than normal, and some historians think Egyptian workers probably used them to move heavy stone blocks into place while building the pyramids.

Crane

The ancient Greeks were the first people to use cranes on building sites. More than 2,500 years ago these were operated by people and donkeys and could lift a block of stone weighing up to 1,000 pounds. The technology was later improved by Roman military engineers who built a much larger version called the Polyspastos. This could lift several tons and required three ropes, five pulleys, and four men to operate it.

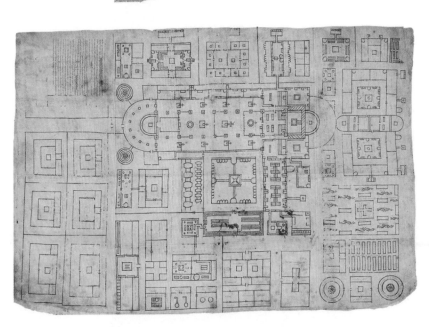

Architectural plans

Switzerland's Plan of Saint Gall is the oldest known architectural drawing on parchment, a type of writing material made from animal skin. It is approximately 1,200 years old and shows a series of medieval monastery buildings with over 300 handwritten inscriptions. The plan includes various chapels, houses, stables, kitchens, workshops, a hospital and even a brewery for making beer. These would have been large enough to accommodate nearly 400 people but unfortunately nothing was ever built.

Going underground

Many of the strangest and most fascinating structures are subterranean. People choose to build underground for many different reasons. It might be convenience, or for defense, or sometimes simply when all the space above ground has already been built on.

11. The Eleven Rock Churches of Lalibela (Ethiopia, 12th century)

These extraordinary Christian churches were built on the orders of a late twelfth century king, who wanted to attract religious pilgrims to this wild and mountainous part of east Africa. Each of his churches was cut from a single block of solid red granite beneath ground level. Many years were then spent carving into the blocks to hollow out their interiors and make openings for windows and doors. The finished churches are up to 50 feet tall but because each one is hidden in a deep trench, there is very little to see when walking through the surrounding landscape.

12. Roman Catacombs (Italy, 2nd century)

Rome is the site of many of Europe's most spectacular ancient ruins. The catacombs include more than 20 miles of dark chambers and winding passageways, which were carved out of volcanic rock by Romans. The work took more than 300 years, beginning in the second century, and the chambers were then used as burial places for Rome's dead. Early Christians also used to meet among the tombs to pray in secret at a time when their religion was illegal, until an emperor called Constantine in the fourth century made Christianity the official religion across the whole of the Roman Empire.

13. Zeljava Air Base (Croatia, 1968)

This secret military airport is hidden inside Plješivica, a mountain on the border of Croatia and Bosnia-Herzegovina. It was constructed during a period called the Cold War (1947–89) when western Europe and the United States felt threatened by Russia and the communist countries of eastern Europe. No actual war broke out in Europe but both sides spent huge sums of money strengthening their military forces and spying on each other. Željava had room for 1,000 troops and could shelter as many as 80 jet fighters from a possible nuclear attack.

14. Dìxià Chéng (China, 1960s)

The world's largest air-raid shelter was constructed beneath Beijing in the 1960s when it looked like China and Russia might go to war. The shelter covered around 33 square miles (that's more than a thousand soccer fields) and had nearly 100 entrances at street level, which were cleverly disguised to look like ordinary shops. It was built so that hundreds of thousands of Chinese citizens could live underground for several months if they needed to. It included restaurants, schools, theaters, factories, hospitals, and even an underground farm for growing mushrooms.

15. Straining Tower (UK, 1880s)

The largest lake in Wales looks natural but is actually human-made. Lake Vyrnwy was created in the 1880s by flooding an entire valley after the people living in it had been ordered to relocate to a new village built for them. Their houses are still there today, hidden beneath almost 16 billion gallons of water, but the lake's most famous feature is the little Straining Tower, which sticks up above the surface. This looks like a fairy castle but it conceals some ingenious Victorian engineering and two huge iron and steel pipes. Each one is more than 60 miles long and in parts large enough for a horse to walk through. Together they carry more than 50 million gallons of fresh water every day to the people of Liverpool, England.

16. London Underground (UK, 1863)

The world's first underground passenger railway sold 30,000 tickets when it opened on January 10, 1863. Many Victorians found trains scary to start. Now more than 250 miles of track carry 543 electric trains through 272 stations. Although no one has ever counted them, its huge network of tunnels is home to approximately half a million tiny mice and a type of mosquito that thrives in underground subways. The station nearest the British Museum is rumored to be haunted by the ghost of an Egyptian mummy, and the deepest one was opened and then closed permanently before a single passenger had even used it.

Monumental statues

In London on New Year's Eve 1853, a celebratory dinner was held inside a sculpture of a dinosaur. The model of the prehistoric iguanodon was large enough for nearly two dozen scientists to sit down to eat, but there are many statues around the world that are even larger, much older—and a lot more famous.

17. The Great Sphinx of Giza
(Egypt, 2500 BCE)

One of the largest stone carvings in the world is as tall as a seven-story building and more than 4,500 years old. The mythical beast it represents has the body of a lion and a human head, with eyes that are nearly six feet in diameter. Its face looks east into the sunrise and some say the statue was positioned to guard the Great Pyramid of Pharaoh Khufu. Originally it was bright red with a yellow headdress, but the wind and sand have gradually worn the paint away so that today the stone blends into the desert landscape. The creature's face has also lost its huge nose, which may have been broken off in the fourteenth century by someone who disapproved of local farmers worshipping the statue.

18. Easter Island (Rapa Nui) (Chile, 1400s)

A tiny volcanic island hundreds of miles out in the Pacific Ocean is home to almost 1,000 gigantic stone statues. These were carved by the Rapa Nui people who called them *mo'ai*. Some of them are more than a thousand years old but no one knows who the statues are meant to be or what they were for. Mo'ai were clearly very important to the Rapa Nui, however, and some historians think they spent so much time and effort creating them that they used up the natural resources of the entire island. When this happened, the islanders ran out of food.

19. Christ the Redeemer (Brazil, 1931)

This 100-foot-high statue looks even larger than it is because it stands on the summit of Mount Corcovado, almost half a mile above the city of Rio de Janeiro. It was built of reinforced concrete in the 1920s, completed in 1931, and is covered in six million triangular stone tiles. The workers who fixed these tiles in place are believed to have written secret messages on the back of many of them, but these are still hidden a hundred years later. An electric train and long escalators carry more than two million visitors a year up to the statue, where there is a small chapel for couples wishing to get married, before making the journey back down again.

20. Statue of Liberty
(USA, 1876)

The USA's largest statue was a gift from the people of France. It arrived in New York in 1885 as 350 giant pieces packed into 214 wooden boxes. Since the pieces were put together, the statue's copper skin has turned green with age and been struck by lightning at least 80,000 times. New Yorkers call it Lady Liberty and, at 305 feet tall, she was often the first thing many European immigrants saw when they arrived by ship to start a new life in the USA. The statue's big toes are the size of a four-year old child and its gigantic 25 foot sandals are the largest in existence.

Defensive structures

From Iron Age forts and medieval castles to subterranean hide-outs and sophisticated early warning systems, the history of warfare has produced many truly magnificent structures, as well as some of the strangest and most sinister-looking ones you will ever see.

21. **Windsor Castle** (UK, 11th century)

The world's oldest and largest castle that is still lived in, Windsor has been an important stronghold for nearly a thousand years and a favorite home of kings and queens since Norman times. In the sixteenth century, Queen Elizabeth I took refuge at the castle when plague swept through London, and Elizabeth II slept in one of its dungeons as a young girl during World War II. The castle has more than a thousand rooms and so many antique clocks (at least 400) that a person is employed full time to wind them up and keep them running. The fourteenth century kitchen is the oldest working one in Britain and the cook's clock is set to be five minutes fast so that His Majesty's meals are never late.

22. Krak des Chevaliers
(Syria, 12th century)

Beginning in the eleventh century, enormous armies marched hundreds of miles across Europe and West Asia to expel all Muslims from Jerusalem and the Holy Land in a series of terrible religious wars called the Crusades. These lasted more than 200 years and cost millions of lives. In the end, the Christian armies were defeated but they left behind several important fortifications, including this immense twelfth century fortress. It was large enough to house 2,000 troops who managed to survive around a dozen well-organized attacks by a much larger well-organised Muslim army. Unfortunately for the troops, the knights were tricked into surrendering by a clever military commander called Sultan Baybars, and the castle was lost.

23. Ksar of Aït Benhaddou
(Morocco, 11th century)

A *ksar* is an Arabic word for a fortified village rather than a castle, and the one at Aït Benhaddou was built on an important trade route across the Sahara desert. The original settlement was constructed in the eleventh century although none of the buildings we see today are more than 300 years old. The most attractive ones are made of sun-dried clay bricks called adobe. The people built the houses clustered together as a way of protecting themselves from attack, but life in the desert is hard so there are now only a few families left.

24. Maunsell Sea Forts
(UK, 1940s)

Looking like giant robot insects striding through the waves, these heavily armed towers were built in the Thames and Mersey estuaries to defend London and Liverpool from attack during World War II. The forts were equipped with powerful searchlights and anti-aircraft guns and their crews successfully shot down nearly two dozen enemy aircraft and about 30 deadly flying bombs known as "doodlebugs." After the war, two of the forts were destroyed when ships crashed into them and a third was wrecked in a violent storm. Most of the others are now derelict and falling apart, although there is a campaign to rescue some of them before it is too late.

25. Maginot Line (France, 1930s)

After the German army launched a devastating surprise attack on France in 1914, the French government decided to build a 280-mile-long series of defenses to stop it happening again. These included underground forts, armored bunkers, and machine-gun posts along the countries' shared border. An underground railroad was constructed to move weapons and ammunition to where they were needed most, and accommodation was provided for thousands of well-trained troops. More than 150 gun turrets were hidden below ground and could be made to pop up in the event of an attack. This highly advanced system took six years to complete and the fortifications looked impregnable. Unfortunately, the next time the Germans attacked, in May 1940, its soldiers ignored the Maginot Line completely and marched into France through Belgium and Holland instead. The French surrendered the following month.

26. Great Wall (China, 700 BCE)

People used to believe the world's longest human-made structure could be seen from space, but it can't, although it is more than 13,000 miles from end to end. Parts of it are 2,300 years old but much of the wall was built during the Ming period (1368 to 1644). At that time prisoners were forced to work on it as a punishment and used sticky rice flour as a form of cement. The wall was meant to keep China's enemies out, but it wasn't entirely successful. The country was conquered twice, once by the Mongol people and then again by the powerful Manchu army. On this second occasion, a traitor in China's own army deliberately left a gateway open in the wall so that the enemy's troops could rush through.

27. Duga-2 (Siberia, 1970s)

In the 1970s, both Russia and the United States—the world's two military superpowers—expected to be attacked by each other. Their governments spent billions of dollars on nuclear weapons and sophisticated electronic networks to warn if an attack was about to be launched. The Russian system was called Duga and it took the form of two huge, rectangular metal radar antennae more than 2,300 feet long and 500 feet tall. These were hidden in remote forests to stop the Americans trying to destroy them and the system was reportedly powerful enough to detect a single aircraft or nuclear missile more than 1,500 miles away.

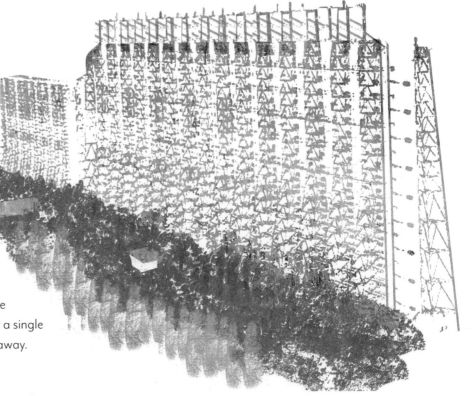

The builders

The first huts used as homes were simple structures that ordinary men and women built for themselves. For thousands of years there were no professional builders or building designers. Expert builders – the skilled stonemasons, the engineers, and architects – only began working much later on. They were only needed as buildings grew larger and more sophisticated.

The Roman army

The Romans built 50,000 miles of new, straight roads as well as towns and cities in the countries they conquered and long stone aqueducts to keep the cities' populations supplied with fresh water. The building work was often supervised by army engineers who did such a good job that many of their roads are still used today. Hundreds of Roman buildings have also survived and examples can be found in more than 40 countries. Although many are ruins, the stonework is of such high quality that it is still standing after more than 2,000 years. The largest survivor is Hadrian's Wall in the north of England, which originally stretched across the entire country—around 75 miles from coast to coast.

Cathedral of St John's, 's-Hertogenbosch, Netherlands

Medieval stonemasons

For centuries, the tallest buildings in Europe were its cathedrals and abbeys. Their towers and spires could be more than 300 feet tall so building them required a lot of expertise. The work was carried out by stonemasons rather than architects or engineers. Many of them couldn't read or write so they worked by experimenting with new ideas, or what we call trial and error. If a new idea worked they passed the knowledge on to younger masons, often their own children, by showing them how it was done. Masons were also responsible for carving blocks of stone into ornate shapes to create the breathtaking interiors that make these some of the most beautifully decorated buildings anywhere in the world.

Renaissance architects

In the fifteenth and sixteenth centuries, people began to study the building methods that had been used by the ancient Greeks and Romans nearly 2,000 years earlier. Professional architects started to design buildings in a similar style, which is now known as Classical architecture. Having seen how long some of the Greek and Roman buildings had lasted, they took a much more scientific approach to their construction rather than just trying something and hoping it wouldn't fall down. These architects drew detailed plans for builders to follow and sometimes made scale models to show what a building would look like when it was completed.

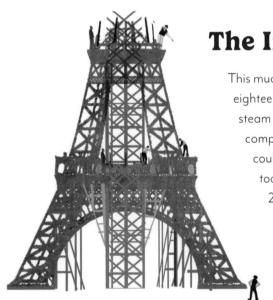

The Industrial Revolution

This much more technological approach continued into the eighteenth and nineteenth century, by which time powerful steam engines could be used to manufacture thousands of components that fitted together perfectly. Huge buildings could be built faster than ever before, and by 1889 it took only two years to join 18,038 metal girders using 2,500,000 rivets to make the Eiffel Tower. Fewer than 300 people were needed to build the world's tallest man-made structure, compared to the tens of thousands of ancient Egyptians who built the pyramids.

Prefab homes

Ordinary people can still build their own homes today, as they did thousands of years ago. However, for many of them this is now only possible because entire houses can be bought as a kit. South Korea is one of several countries where factories are turning out the components that make building a home faster and easier than ever before. Doing it this way can save money and might help to solve the housing crisis, which affects many younger people.

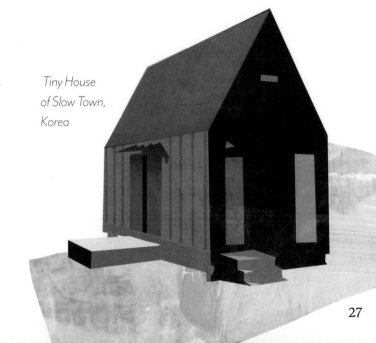

Tiny House of Slow Town, Korea

Palaces of power

Built to impress friends and enemies alike, humans have constructed incredible buildings to show the wealth and accomplishments of their country. From their amazing gardens, to their huge rooms and inspiring art, palaces and castles have been a popular choice for any ruler keen to hold on to power.

28. Versailles (France, 17th century)

The extravagance of the French royal family led to a revolution in 1789. Versailles, Europe's largest and most luxurious palace, was the most visible symbol of their greed and overspending. Surrounded by 45 square miles of private gardens (and 1,400 fountains), its hundreds of glittering, candle-lit rooms were the setting for elaborate court ceremonies and lavish parties. Taxes had been raised repeatedly to spend on luxuries, even though many ordinary French people couldn't afford to feed their children. The revolutionaries put the king and queen in prison and then had them beheaded. Versailles was abandoned, cast aside as a hated place that no one wanted. The palace lay empty for years until it became a museum that now attracts nearly 10 million visitors a year.

29. Buda Castle (Hungary, 18th century)

The city of Budapest was originally three separate towns called Buda, Óbuda, and Pest and is dominated by a large and magnificent walled castle. Its rich decorations (in a style called Baroque) make it look like it was built in the eighteenth century but most of it is much newer, as the castle had to be rebuilt after being virtually destroyed in World War II. Earlier fortresses on the site were similarly ransacked by invaders, gutted by fire, blown up, and eventually allowed just to fall down. Even when Queen Maria Theresa spent a fortune building this one, she had already decided she didn't want to live in the castle, so it became a nunnery and later a university. Despite all this, Buda Castle is still hugely important to the Hungarian people and its survival into the twenty-first century is seen as a glorious symbol of Hungary's complex and often difficult history.

30. Alhambra
(Spain, 13th century)

Spain was invaded in the eighth century by Muslims known as Moors, who ruled most of the country for the next 700 years. This was a golden era for Islamic art and architecture, and the richly decorated buildings, courtyards, and ornamental pools of the Alhambra make it one of the finest examples. High defensive walls and massive towers conceal the spectacular hilltop palace of the Moorish rulers. It took a series of battles to drive them out in 1492 and then Spain's new Catholic king and queen took over the Alhambra. They altered many of the buildings but what remains of the medieval Islamic decor is still its best and most striking feature. Fabulous colors and complex geometric patterns cover almost every surface in a dazzling display of carved stone, ornate plasterwork, handmade tiles, and exotic woods from around the world. This blend of eastern and western styles is very unusual and makes the Alhambra one of Spain's most widely admired structures.

31. Jag Niwas
(India, 18th century)

For centuries, the country called India was made up of hundreds of separate kingdoms. These could be as small as a few square miles and were ruled by maharajas and occasionally by female maharanis. Many of these rulers built themselves beautiful palaces, such as this extraordinary example, which appears to float on Lake Pichola in the state of Udaipur. It belonged to Jagat Singh II, who ruled this part of India from 1734 to 1751. Jagat Singh had the marble-walled palace built in honor of Surya, the Hindu sun god, which is why it faces east into the sunrise, although it is now a hotel. The building's unusual location keeps it cool in the summer months when temperatures can soar to 120°F or more.

32. The Forbidden City
(China, 15th century)

China hasn't had an emperor for more than a hundred years, but it still has the largest royal palace in the world. This occupies nearly one thousand different buildings, which are all surrounded by high walls and a deep moat in the middle of Beijing. Most of them are built of wood and they contain so many rooms (8,886 altogether) that if you visited one room a day, every day, it would take you more than 24 years to see them all. Most of the buildings are painted red and all but two have bright yellow roof tiles. These were important colors in Imperial China and reserved for the emperor. This meant ordinary Chinese people and even important officials were never allowed to wear clothes of either color.

33. Gyantse Dzongc
(Tibet, 14th century)

One of the most astonishingly positioned structures in the whole of Asia was built more than a thousand years ago in the high mountains of southern Tibet. It became a royal residence in the 14th century for Kungpa Phakpa, the son of a powerful prince. Gyantse Dzong's lonely position at the top of rock cliffs made it very difficult to attack, although British soldiers eventually captured it in 1904. They were able to do this by blowing a hole in the wall, which hit a store of ammunition, ripping an even larger hole in the main defensive wall. Today a steep, winding footpath goes right to the top of the rock on which the castle stands. The views from the walls are spectacular but the air is so thin that, at nearly 4,000 metres above sea level, it is a hard climb for many visitors.

Reaching for the Sky

People have always been fascinated by really tall structures. These can be used to show the wealth and power of building owners and even entire countries, or to demonstrate the technical genius of the architects and engineers who designed them. Throughout history the urge to build higher and higher has never gone away, although the form and function of the buildings themselves have changed many times over the centuries.

34. Ulm Minster
(Germany, 14th century)

161.5 m

Religious buildings are often built to impress the people who worship in them, and for a long time the world's tallest structures were the towers and soaring spires of the great churches and cathedrals of Europe. Builders started working on Ulm Minster in the Middle Ages, but it wasn't completed until the late 19th century, where eventually it was topped by the tallest spire in the world at 161.5 metres. Visitors can go almost to the top if they don't mind climbing 768 steps, but the Minster could soon be overtaken by a church in the Spanish city of Barcelona. The huge Sagrada Familia was begun nearly 150 years ago but is still not finished. Its designer wanted a total of eighteen spires and, by 2026 according to the latest estimate, the huge cross positioned on the top of the main spire will reach an astonishing 172.5 metres into the air.

35. Empire State Building (USA, 1930s)

In the 1930s, office buildings and apartment blocks known as skyscrapers began to dominate city skylines, especially in America. These were built using the most up to date techniques, such as strong steel skeletons instead of thick walls of brick or stone. At one point, the country could boast that it had 99 of the world's 100 tallest buildings, including the very tallest one. This was New York's 380 metre Empire State Building, which held on to the record for 40 years. It was possible to see six of America's 50 states from the top. A race developed between New York and Chicago to see which city could build the biggest skyscraper of all.

380 m

The Empire State Building is the 9th tallest building in the USA.

36. NASA Vehicle Assembly Building
(USA, 1960s)

The world's tallest skyscrapers can now have more than 150 storeys but this super-tall structure is unique because it has only one. As the name suggests, it is where NASA builds its space rockets, in Florida's Kennedy Space Center – including the gigantic Apollo/Saturn V, which carried the first astronauts to the Moon and back. In the 1960s, this rocket was the largest, most powerful rocket ever made so it needed an even more gigantic building. The VAB is so big that rain clouds sometimes form inside it, and more than 2,300 litres of paint were needed to create the giant American flag painted on its side. Its doors are the four largest doors ever manufactured – it takes 45 minutes to open them – and the interior of the building is so huge that you could squeeze nearly 1,500 Olympic-sized swimming pools inside.

1,000 m
(predicted)

160 m

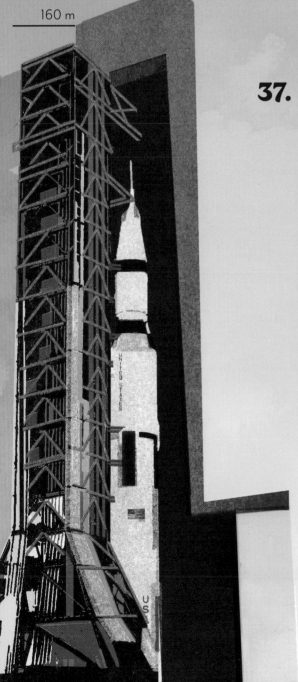

37. Jeddah Tower
(Saudi Arabia)

Jeddah Tower is expected to be more than a kilometre high when it is finished, although no one knows yet when this will be. Its enormous size poses all sorts of technical problems, not just in the way it is built (it is four times taller than the world's highest crane) but also in ensuring it can survive very strong winds. Modern buildings do this by swaying from side to side slightly, but this can be very uncomfortable for the people inside. To prevent anyone feeling seasick, the needle-like tower has been designed to be as aerodynamic as possible, and its unusual triangular footprint makes it even more stable.

The current record for the tallest skyscraper is held by the Burj Khalifa in Dubai at 829.9 m – almost six times taller than the Pyramid of Khufu.

Religious Structures

Many of the world's most remarkable structures are ones that were built as a place of worship, or to glorify gods and significant religious figures. Many ancient religions are not well understood by historians because the civilisations connected to them have died out. In some of these cases, the ruins left behind are the only evidence we have that the people who lived thousands of years ago had any religious beliefs at all.

38. Stonehenge (UK, 2500 bce)

There are more than a thousand prehistoric stone circles in the British Isles, but Stonehenge in Wiltshire is the largest and easily the most famous. It was built in stages, beginning 5,000 years ago, using heavy stone brought from as far away as Wales. It once formed the centrepiece of vast area of temples, tombs and other Bronze Age structures but its original purpose is still not well understood. The careful positioning of the great stones, however, suggests that its creators were probably interested in the way the sun moved across the sky throughout each year. We know that sun worship formed an important part of many early religions and farmers have known for thousands of years that the sun's energy is important for growing crops. This could certainly explain why so much effort was spent moving, shaping and erecting more than twenty tonnes of stone to create this incredible monument.

39. Parthenon
(Greece, 5th century BCE)

The ancient Greeks worshipped twelve main gods and approximately 400 minor ones. Because of this they had thousands of temples, including the Parthenon, which was built high above the city of Athens in the fifth century BCE. The temple is dedicated to the goddess Athena and built mostly of limestone and marble. It has a total of 50 columns supporting the roof and its design has been copied many times. The Parthenon is still regarded as one of the most beautiful buildings of all time, even though much of it was destroyed in the seventeenth century. Later on, to the anger of many Greeks today, its finest carvings were taken from the ruins and put on display in the British Museum.

40. The Western Wall
(Jerusalem, 19 BCE)

Jewish people worship only one god and their holiest temple was destroyed more than 2,000 years ago by the Romans who ruled Jerusalem at that time. A 65-foot-high, 160-foot-long stretch of wall survived and has become an important place of pilgrimage, where Jewish people pray —one of their prayers being for the temple to be rebuilt. Their prayers are often written down on small pieces of paper and inserted into the cracks between the wall's huge stone blocks. It is possible to access a series of tunnels containing archaeological discoveries, including large stone arches and part of a Roman aqueduct.

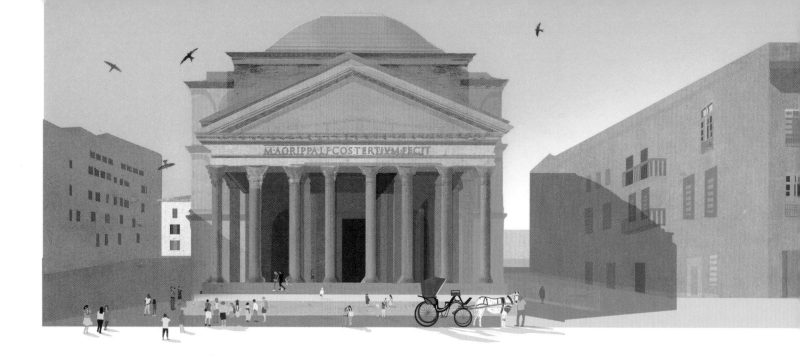

41. Pantheon
(Italy, 125 CE)

The Romans invented concrete by mixing volcanic ash and seawater. This was strong enough for it to be used to construct the ancient world's widest dome on top of this circular temple, dedicated to all the Roman gods. The immense building is still in use today as a Catholic church. Worshippers sometimes get wet as rain falls through a large circular hole in the dome, called the *oculus*, a Latin word meaning "eye." This lets in sunlight as well as rain (which drains away through special channels in the stone floor), and may have been used to tell the time, by observing the sunlight from inside the building as it moved around the high curved walls.

42. Sri Harmandir Sahib
(India, 17th century)

The most important Sikh temple, or *gurdwara*, is known as the Golden Temple because its marble and copper exterior is covered in hundreds of pounds of pure gold. It combines Hindu and Muslim architectural styles and is visited by around 100,000 people every day. Many of them receive a free vegetarian meal after praying, which is produced by Sikh volunteers in the temple's own *langar*, or kitchen. The temple has four entrances and a ceiling studded with precious jewels, but visitors first have to cross the enormous square lake that surrounds it. The most devout or religious Sikhs take a dip in the lake before praying at the temple.

The lake is filled with water from the nearby Ravi River.

43. Hagia Sophia
(Turkey, 6th century)

This was built in an architectural style called Byzantine. Its cavernous interior made it the largest building on Earth at that time, and other builders soon began to copy the clever way in which its large circular dome was made to fit on top of a square building. To begin with, Hagia Sophia was a Christian cathedral, but it became a mosque after the region was conquered by a Muslim sultan called Mehmed II. Although the worshippers today are all Muslims, its fabulous mosaic decorations still include images of Jesus, his mother Mary, and various Christian saints.

Coping with climate change

It took until the twentieth century for anyone to realize that the pollution from burning natural resources such as wood, peat, and coal was damaging our planet. Scientists started looking for more environmentally friendly sources of power, but there are no easy answers. Even the "greenest" energy requires gigantic new structures to be built, often in wild and beautiful places.

44. Ekibastuz Gres-2
(Kazakhstan, 1987)

The tallest chimney ever built can be seen from many miles away. It is made of concrete and, at almost 1,378 feet high, it's about the same as a 130-story skyscraper. The chimney forms part of an old-fashioned power station called Ekibastuz, which can generate enough energy to heat nearly a million homes—but only by burning enormous amounts of coal from one of the world's largest mines next door. It means it's cheap to buy but burning coal like this is highly polluting and extremely damaging to wildlife.

45. Mojave Wind Farm
(USA, 2010)

Wind is one of the most popular sources of clean, renewable energy, especially in places where it blows nearly every day. Converting wind into electricity is expensive and requires giant windmills called turbines. These can be built on land or out at sea, and often hundreds at a time are clustered together to form something called a wind farm. Mojave is the USA's largest wind farm, containing 600 tall white turbines, each 2,625 feet high. Many people enjoy watching the blades turn slowly in the wind, but others regard the towers as eyesores, and birds are often killed or injured if they fly too close.

46. Three Gorges Dam
(China, 2016)

Water or hydroelectric power is another excellent source of clean energy and uses a different sort of turbine that spins when water rushes past the blades instead of air. The world's largest scheme is on the Yangtze River in China. More than a million people had to leave their homes to make way for a vast new reservoir. However, the result is astonishing. The reservoir itself is 410 miles from end to end and the water in it is held back by a dam that is more than 330 feet thick.

Thousands of gallons of water pass through dozens of turbines every second to generate enough power for two cities the size of London.

47. Bhadla Solar Park
(India, 2020)

Many houses have a few shiny black solar panels on the roof but at Bhadla more than 10 million of them have been used to cover 22 square miles of scorching hot Indian desert. The panels convert sunshine into electricity without producing any harmful emissions, and India not the country has built dozens of these solar parks to make the most of its sunny climate. Bhadla is the largest one anywhere in the world and is already generating nearly five times more power than dirty Ekibastuz and its famous chimney.

48. Chernobyl's Coffin
(Ukraine, 1986)

Nuclear power plants generate electricity by splitting atoms, the tiny particles that make up all the matter in the universe. This process is so efficient that more power can be obtained from the atoms in two pounds of uranium (a type of radioactive metal) than by burning 11 *million* pounds of coal. But if something goes wrong, the results can be horrifying. When this power plant exploded in 1986, a deadly cloud of radioactive material was released into the atmosphere. At least 360,000 people had to be evacuated immediately from their homes and, even today, noone is allowed to move back into the area. The damaged power plant had to be encased in a giant concrete "coffin" but the land around it is still too contaminated for anyone to live there.

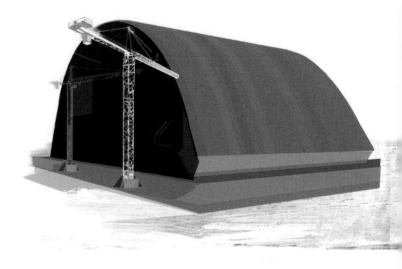

Change of use

When a building is no longer used for its original purpose, it doesn't have to be torn down or abandoned. All around the world buildings have been converted into something brand new, such as shopping malls that have become schools, schools that have been turned into apartment blocks, and old churches that are now libraries, concert halls, recording studios, and even swimming pools.

Grain silos

Tall enough to store hundreds of tons of ripened wheat and other crops, several old farm silos are now used as indoor mountaineering centers. Their slippery metal walls are a challenge for even the most avid climber.

Airship hangars

In the 1930s, airships were the largest moving structures ever built and the hangars built to house them are some of the most enormous buildings you'll ever see. One at Krausnick in Germany has been converted into a tropical paradise —a vast indoor water park complete with swimming pools, islands, palm trees, flumes, and sandy beaches.

Churches

Europe has more than half a million religious buildings, including many that are no longer used for worship. Historic buildings like these are often too important to demolish so are put to different uses—one in Spain has been made into an indoor skate park and another is a university computing center. In the Netherlands, three more have become an enormous bookshop, a trampolining center, and brewery with its own bar.

Bank vaults

Bank vaults are usually constructed deep underground and are protected by heavy steel doors. New uses for old ones include a school library, a small subterranean cinema, wine and whisky bars, and an unusual art gallery.

A material world

A wide variety of different materials have been used to build different structures around the world. The most successful ones, such as wood, brick, and stone have been used for thousands of years—and are still in use today. Builders and architects are still experimenting, however, and today some of the most extraordinary structures on the planet have been assembled— somehow—out of some of the most unexpected stuff.

49. Jukkasjärvi Icehotel
(Sweden, 1989)

This spectacular construction, 125 miles north of the Arctic Circle, must be rebuilt every winter because by April it begins to melt! Giant blocks of snow and ice are pulled from the nearby Torne River and used to build the hotel, along with almost everything inside it. This includes all the tables and chairs, the decorative sculptures, the hotel's ice chapel, its ice bar, and the glasses that the guests drink from. Even the beds are blocks of ice, which is why everyone staying in the hotel is provided with a warm sleeping bag and some reindeer skins to lie on.

50. Great Mosque of Djenné (Mali, 1907)

Although people have been building with mud for centuries, the world's largest mud structure was completed not much more than hundred years ago. The Great Mosque in western Africa is huge: 300 feet long and 130 feet wide, and its walls are made of *ferey*. This is a traditional African brick made by baking wet earth in the hot sun. Each brick is cylindrical rather than the rectangular shape, and once the mud has been baked hard, the bricks are strong enough to build towers more than 50 feet high. Ferey gets damaged by heavy rainfall, but when this happens skilled local craftspeople quickly repair the surface with more sun-dried mud.

51. Palacio de Sal
(Bolivia, 2007)

More than a million blocks of salt were used to make the floors, walls, and ceilings of this extraordinary hotel in South America. In ancient times, salt was almost as valuable as gold because it could only be found in certain places and all humans need salt to live. One of those places is Bolivia, where vast lakes slowly dry out over thousands of years to create desert areas. When this happens, it leaves behind a hard, thick layer of salt. The Salar de Uyuni salt flat contains so much salt that using it as building material makes perfect sense. It also explains why a special cement was created for the hotel by grinding up even more salt and mixing it with water to make the sticky paste needed to hold the million blocks together.

52. New Jerusalem Children's Home
(South Africa, 2011)

A big truck is a common sight on long journeys, and usually its cargo is packed inside a large metal box called a shipping container. Several million of these are used every day to carry goods around the world, by sea, road, and rail. The containers sometimes get damaged but these can be put to a good use instead of being scrapped. The New Jerusalem is a fantastic example of recycling: it is built almost entirely of old containers. They are strong (and very cheap) and now more than two dozen of them provide a safe and cozy new home for 80 South African orphans.

53. Wat Pa Maha Chedi Kaew
(Thailand, 1986)

The buildings that make up this eco-friendly temple were built using 1.5 million empty beer bottles, which some Buddhist monks began collecting in the mid-1980s. The monks wanted to prevent the bottles ending up in a landfill site and found they could save a lot of money by building with what was basically trash. Light filtering through the emerald-green and brown glass bottles produces wonderful patterns on the walls inside, where thousands of metal bottle caps have been used to make mosaiclike patterns.

54. Zhangjiajie Glass Bridge
(China, 2016)

Would you like to walk on a slippery sheet of glass suspended more than 1,000 feet above the ground? Every day thousands of tourists flock to this spectacular structure, which uses more than a hundred thick glass panels to span a canyon between two high cliffs. Zhangjiajie is the longest of China's many glass bridges and "skywalks" and according to its Israeli architect, the panels used to build it are strong enough to support 800 visitors at a time. Taking that first step onto it must still be terrifying though, especially as the bridge also includes China's highest bungee jump for anyone brave enough to jump off.

55. Ithaa Restaurant
(Maldives, 2005)

Explorers who would rather go down instead of up should head for Rangali in the Maldives. The island has a hotel with a restaurant 15 feet under the sea! The tables are arranged inside a pod of transparent acrylic, a type of strong plastic that looks like glass. At Ithaa it's the only thing between the guests and the sharks and stingrays and other colorful creatures that swim in this part of the Indian Ocean. Scuba divers are employed to ensure the acrylic is kept clean and the menu includes vegetarian dishes for anyone who prefers watching fish to eating them.

Famous landmarks

Landmark buildings can be old or new, beautiful or ugly. They can also be much loved by visitors and the people who live nearby—or feared and despised, like a prison or the palace of a tyrant. Most are instantly recognizable, and many have become important symbols of the countries in which they stand.

56. Sydney Opera House (Australia, 1973)

Australia's most famous structure was designed in 1956 by a Danish architect, Jørn Utzon, who won a competition that attracted more than 230 entries. Its highly distinctive roof is made of fourteen huge concrete shells. These have been compared to everything from the wings of a bird to pieces of orange peel and they would form a perfect sphere if all fourteen were removed and rearranged. The first performance at the opera house was given by a famous African-American singer, Paul Robeson, in 1960, who climbed onto one of the shells and stood on the top of it to sing to the workers helping to finish the building.

57. St. Michael of the Needle
(France, 969 CE)

This small church sits on the summit of an extraordinary rock formation, which is all that remains of an ancient volcano. It was built more than a thousand years ago, although the site was already occupied before this. Constructing the church was incredibly difficult because all the materials and the tools had to be hauled to the top by hand before construction work could even begin. Reaching the chapel is slightly easier today thanks to a flight of 268 steps cut into the rock, and benches along the way so visitors can stop and rest.

58. Leaning Tower of Pisa
(Italy, 12th century)

Italy's most famous tower leans so far over it looks as if it's about to fall down. It was built in the twelftth century and began leaning almost immediately because the ground beneath it was too soft. Hundreds of years later the lean is so bad that the eighth story is 15 feet to one side of where it should be. In the sixteenth century, the scientist Galileo is believed to have climbed to the top so he could drop two cannonballs of different weights to see if they would fall at different speeds. His experiment was repeated 400 years later by an astronaut on the Moon. David Scott's hammer and feather hit the ground at exactly the same time because there is no air on the Moon to slow them down.

59. Atomium (Belgium, 1958)

This amazingly futuristic structure was built to look like a crystallized iron molecule that has been magnified 165 billion times. The atoms are represented by huge stainless steel spheres, connected to the central tower by tubes containing some of Europe's longest escalators. Several of the spheres are used as museum or exhibition spaces and the one at the top has a restaurant with fantastic views over the city of Brussels. The whole thing is beautifully illuminated after dark using nearly 3,000 LEDs.

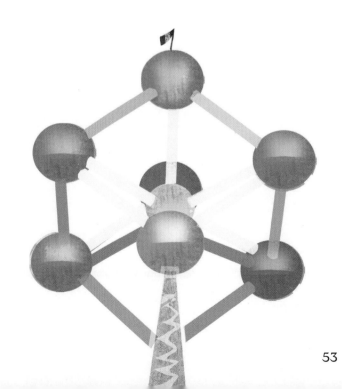

60. Tower Bridge (UK, 1894)

This Victorian bridge was made to look like a medieval castle, which helps it blend in with the Tower of London situated nearby. Despite its old-fashioned appearance, it incorporated many features that were very advanced for the time. A strong steel skeleton was clad in stone and giant steam engines helped lift two sections of roadway each time a large ship needed to pass underneath. This still happens an average of two or three times a day, but modern electric power is now used instead of coal and steam. Daredevil pilots have flown between the towers and in the 1950s, a double-decker bus was driving over the bridge when it suddenly began to open. The quick-thinking driver managed to avoid disaster by jumping the bus over the gap and was given the day off as a reward for saving the passengers' lives.

Cars, ships, and trains

The invention of new forms of mechanized transport changed the world and the way people lived. But these high-speed, long-distance machines also required massive changes to the environment and have led to the creation of many new types of structure to help them function effectively.

The fully automated system can stack 250 cars an hour.

61. Dokk1 Robot Park
(Denmark, 2015)

With 1.4 billion motor vehicles in the world, parking in crowded cities has never been harder. Things are forecast to get a lot worse as that number rises, but a parking lot beneath a library in the city of Aarhus could give us one answer to the problem. Vehicles take up much less space when they are neatly parked by robots instead of their owners, and Dokk1 can fit 1,000 cars into the space normally required for 300.

62. Project *HMS Habakkuk*
(Canada, 1940s)

During World War II, the British prime minister, Winston Churchill, met an inventor who wanted to build a fleet of giant aircraft carriers made of ice. The plan sounded bonkers, but water mixed with sawdust freezes to produce an incredibly strong material called pykrete. This floats because ice is lighter than water, and the sawdust stopped it melting so that bullets and even missiles simply bounced off. The vessels were designed to be well over a third of a mile in length, yet would have been cheaper to build than an ordinary steel warship. The hangars below deck would have been large enough to accommodate 300 Spitfires and other aircraft but, by the time the prototype was tested on a lake in Canada, the war was nearly over and the idea was abandoned.

63. Trans-Siberian Railroad (Russia, 1904)

Trains on the world's longest railroad take seven days to travel more than 5,750 miles from Europe into Asia. Building it took 60,000 workers more than two decades (many were criminals hoping to earn a shorter sentence) and for years a special ship was needed to carry the train across Baikal, the world's deepest lake. Today's passengers pass through nearly 90 cities and across eight different time zones. This means that when it's only midnight at the start of the route, people living at the far end of the railway are already getting up for breakfast.

64. Fiat Lingotto Factory (Italy, 1923)

Fiat used this huge car factory to build 80 different types of car and, for more than 50 years, raw materials were delivered to the first floor and completed vehicles drove off the end of the production line up on the fourth. Concrete ramps spiral up from one level to the next, but its most unusual feature is the high-speed racetrack on its roof.

This was where each new Fiat was tested before being sold. The track was never used for an actual race but the sound of engines revving loudly high above the streets of Turin must have been very strange to the people below.

Getting from A to B

Bridges, tunnels, and canals are still some of the largest, most complex and most expensive structures ever built by architects and engineers.

65. Panama Canal
(Panama, 1914)

The Panama Canal is an amazing shortcut for ships sailing between the Atlantic and Pacific oceans. The journey through the canal is about 50 miles, but if it didn't exist crews would have to spend weeks traveling nearly 12,500 miles around the whole of South America. Digging such a long canal through thick rain forests was very difficult—it took more than 30 years to do. Today, the canal can accommodate giant cargo ships and each year over 13,000 vessels pass through it.

66. Rialto Bridge (Italy, 16th century)

This is the most famous bridge in an ancient city that has canals instead of roads. Venice occupies more than 100 small islands in the north of Italy. The people who live on the islands travel around on foot or by boat. The main route through the city is called the Grand Canal and the Rialto Bridge was built so that pedestrians could cross from one side to the other. The high central arch enables even quite large boats to pass beneath it and the ramps leading up to the middle of the bridge are lined with expensive shops.

67. Gotthard Base Tunnels (Switzerland, 2016)

The world's longest and deepest railroad tunnels pass right through the Swiss Alps, Europe's highest mountain range. The two main tunnels are each just over 35 miles in length but they incorporate another 25 miles of smaller subterranean passages and vertical shafts. Excavating all this required the removal of more than 30 million tons of rock by four gigantic tunnel-boring machines, named Sissi, Heidi, Gabi, and Gabi II. On a good day, these monster machines could chew their way through the mountains at a rate of 80 feet a day and it took 17 years to complete the work.

68. Akashi Kaikyo Bridge (Japan, 1998)

This immense suspension bridge is nearly 2.5 miles from end to end and wide enough to carry a six-lane highway. It was constructed to provide a safe crossing over a dangerous sea channel where nearly 500 passengers had drowned in ferry collisions and sinkings. The bridge had to be built to withstand earthquakes (which are quite common in Japan), so 190,000 miles of wire were used to make the strong cables that support it. That's enough to wind around Earth's equator seven and a half times! In 1995, a particularly bad earthquake still managed to shift the two main towers of the bridge by more than four feet. The bridge miraculously survived but each summer the heat causes it to expand by another six feet before shrinking again when the temperature drops.

Reuse and recycle

We've already seen how old shipping containers and even beer bottles can be recycled into building materials. Around the world there are many other examples of things being reused in this way, including entire buildings, which have been cleverly constructed out of what other people just throw away.

Tire home

Between one and two billion car tires are scrapped every year but they are not biodegradable and recycling them is very difficult. One answer is to build with them—although old tires are ugly, they are very strong and hardwearing. They can be filled with mud before building begins (this improves the insulation to keep the house warm) or compressed into bales, a sort of large black rubber building block.

A treehouse from trash

On the Brazilian island of Santa Catarina there is a giant treehouse, large enough to sleep five people. It was built using secondhand bricks, wooden planks, tiles, and even pieces of glass that had been rescued from older buildings when they were demolished.

The bottle school

This children's school in the Philippines is made of old plastic water bottles filled with adobe, or dried mud. These cost virtually nothing and the finished building is actually stronger than one made of bricks and concrete.

The floating island

Joyxee Island in Mexico is an artificial island made of bags containing more than 100,000 plastic bottles full of air. A layer of soil on top of the bags enables tropical vegetation to grow on the surface and the plants' winding roots help keep the island in one piece. A solar-powered three-story house on the island is home to two people and their pet dog.

Wing house

Several old airliners have been converted into homes, but one American took the idea a step further and built himself a brand-new house using airplane parts. Its most obvious feature is a roof made from the wings of a giant Boeing 747. These are light and strong, as well as weatherproof because aluminum doesn't rust. A helicopter was needed to lift them into position but the house was still quite cheap to build. This is because airplanes of this size cost around $25,000,000 when new but a disused one could be bought for only a few thousand.

Places for pleasure

Among the world's most extraordinary structures—old ones as well as these newer examples—are those that were built as places where people can enjoy the serious business of having fun.

69. Narendra Modi Stadium
(India, 2020)

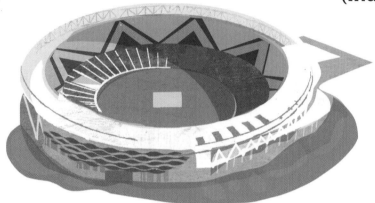

In India, well over a billion people watch cricket regularly, which is far more than in any other country. Unsurprisingly, it has the world's largest sports stadium, a vast circular structure able to seat an incredible 132,000 spectators. Most come to see cricket although games of hockey, soccer, and basketball are also played here. India's largest parking lot is next door but even this has only 13,000 parking spaces, so many fans travel to the games by train, arriving at the stadium's own railroad station.

70. Jebel Jais Flight (UAE, 2018)

The longest zipline on the planet is longer than 28 soccer fields and reaches speeds of up to 95 miles an hour! Anyone brave enough to ride on it must first travel along a steep, winding track to the top of the region's highest mountain before being strapped into a harness and fitted with a safety helmet. The first person to try this was the ruler of Ras Al Khaimah in 2018. As soon as he reached the bottom, he told a television crew that he was *definitely* going to do it again.

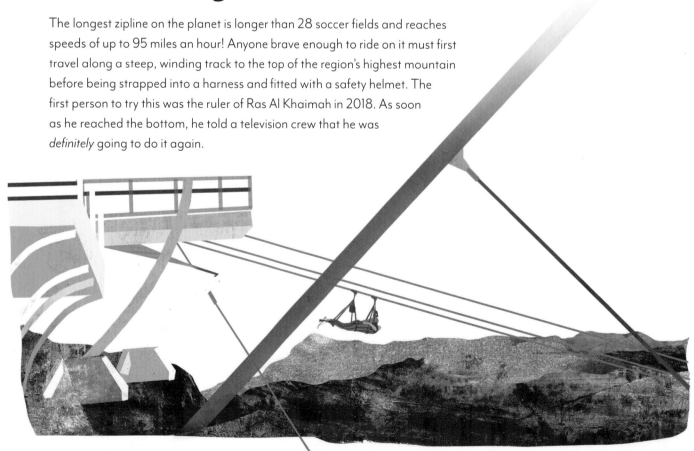

71. A ballroom at the bottom of a lake
(UK, 1890s)

Dancing underwater never really caught on as a hobby, but one small Victorian ballroom has survived beneath a lake in the countryside south of London. It was built for Whitaker Wright, who later poisoned himself after being arrested for stealing hundreds of millions of British pounds from various different companies. His little ballroom was made of cast iron and panes of strong glass that were nearly three inches thick. To reach it, Wright and his guests had to climb down a spiral staircase and walk through a long, dark tunnel running along the bottom of the lake. After Wright's death it was bought by the owner of the company that designed and built the *Titanic*.

72. Deep Dive
(UAE, 2021)

The world's deepest swimming pool in Dubai contains a vast underwater film set designed to look like a genuine sunken city. Divers can descend to a depth of 200 feet while exploring various spooky ruined buildings, graffiti-covered walls, working streetlights, and even an abandoned car. There's an underwater bicycle down there too, for anyone wishing to exercise, and a pool table for divers who want to relax. Dry viewing areas deep underground enable spectators to watch the divers if they are nervous about taking the plunge themselves.

73. Montreal Biosphère
(Canada, 1995)

This enormous transparent bubble was constructed nearly 60 years ago but a disastrous fire almost destroyed it a decade later and it had to be rebuilt. The striking design is an ingenious type of structure called a geodesic dome. These are made of hundreds of plastic triangles set into lightweight steel frames and they are very energy efficient. The Biosphère is one of the largest of these domes ever built and it houses a museum of the environment and the natural world.

74. Formula Rossa
(UAE, 2010)

Famous for building some of the most beautiful and most expensive automobiles ever produced, the Italian supercar maker Ferrari has also had a hand in creating the world's fastest rollercoaster. Passengers riding on the Formula Rossa find out what it feels like to accelerate to a speed of 150 miles per hour in under five seconds. That's less time than it takes a Formula One car to reach the same speed during the grand prix. The record-breaking rollercoaster is also one of the longest in the world but, because it's so fast, each ride lasts just 90 thrilling seconds.

Life after death

The most lavish tombs, especially in ancient times, often needed thousands of workers to build them and could take decades to construct. Now they attract millions of visitors a year to marvel at their size, sophistication, and scale.

75. Taj Mahal (India, 17th century)

The spectacular tomb for a much-loved wife is one of the most photographed buildings anywhere in the world. Shah Jahan was the Muslim ruler of India in the seventeenth century and his beloved Mumtaz Mahal died after giving birth to their fourteenth child. More than 20,000 craftspeople worked on the building with its four tall minarets, or towers,

and gleaming, white marble dome. The spike on the top of the dome (called a *finial*) was originally made of gold but this was replaced by a bronze one in the nineteenth century. Shah Jahan planned to build himself an identical structure in black marble opposite the Taj Mahal but he died before work on it began.

76. Tomb of the Qin Emperor
(China, 200s BCE)

The most amazing discovery made at China's most famous archaeological site is an army of life-size sculptures of around 8,000 soldiers, horses, and chariots. These are made of clay or terracotta and are more than 2,200 years old. The army was created to accompany the dead emperor's journey into the afterlife and the sculptures are so detailed that no two are the same. The soldiers' bodies are identical, but they have different heads, hats, shoes, and even ears and mustaches, so that each one seems to have its own individual character and identity. The tomb itself is enormous, and new discoveries are still being made there after nearly 50 years of digging.

77. Lenin Mausoleum
(Russia, 1930)

A violent revolution in 1917 led to the creation of the world's first communist government. The man in charge was Vladimir Ilich Ulyanov (known as Lenin), who remained in power for the next six years. During this time, many hundreds of thousands of Russians were imprisoned or murdered on his orders, but when he died a huge red mausoleum was built in his honor outside the Kremlin, a former royal palace. Russians still line up to see Lenin's body inside it, which was put on display after being preserved with special chemicals.

78. Shah-i-Zinda
(Uzbekistan, 11th century)

Rich mosaics and stunning turquoise and yellow tiles cover this immense necropolis in the city of Samarqand. The word necropolis means "city of the dead" in Ancient Greek and Shah-i-Zinda has been an important burial place for almost a thousand years. It began as a shrine to Kusam ibn Abbas, a key figure in early Islamic history, as he was the Prophet Muhammad's cousin. Over many centuries, the most powerful families in the region chose to be buried close to his shrine, and today Shah-i-Zinda is one of the most impressive sites in this part of central Asia.

Out of this world

No species has traveled farther than humans or built such strange and daring structures so far from home. Where to next—Mars?

79. Halley VI Research Station
(Antarctica, 2012)

The coldest and most remote inhabited spot on Earth, this bizarre-looking research station is usually home to dozens of scientists and engineers as well as a colony of penguins. This close to the South Pole, there is no daylight for more than a hundred days of the year and the temperature can fall as low as −67°F. Scientists come here to live and study all sorts of things, from climate change to the local wildlife. They stay, often for months at a time, in eight strange four- or six-legged pods. Each one is mounted on skis so it can be dragged (very slowly) from one place to another—in 2017 the entire station had to be moved to prevent it falling through giant cracks that had opened up in the melting ice.

80. International Space Station (Outer Space, 1998)

When the ISS whizzes over your house, it's traveling at 17,000 miles an hour and circling Earth every 90 minutes. This means the crew gets to see 16 sunrises and sunsets every single day. Most of the time the space station is only 250 miles from Earth, or about a third of the distance between those scientists in Antarctica and their nearest village or town. It's an amazing structure, however, and not just because it's one of the fastest ever built. Inside it's about the same size as a six-bedroom house (with a couple of bathrooms and even a gym), so it's easily large enough to see at night. The solar panels that power it are huge and because nothing this large could be launched in one piece, more than 40 separate missions were needed to carry everything up by rocket to build the ISS out in space. So far, almost 250 people from nearly 20 different countries have spent time on board, and the record stay is an incredible 665 days.

What will we build next?

Whether you're in Antarctica or outer space, the sheer variety of different structures designed and created by humans is incredible. From mosques of mud to bridges of glass, from skyscrapers to secret subterranean hideouts, from billion-dollar towers to an island made of recycled waste—it's hard to imagine what human ingenuity will come up with next.

The way we live

Already there are plans to construct buildings on the Moon and even on Mars, but here on Earth changes to the way we live now are affecting the type of structures being built. Worries about the environment are certain to have an impact because buildings already account for nearly half of all greenhouse gas emissions and at least half of all the energy produced from fossil fuels and sustainable sources, such as solar and wind. In the future, buildings will have to be smarter, cleaner, and more efficient.

Smarter construction

People travel much farther and more often than in the past, so new transport networks will be needed for machines like China's new superfast magnetic levitation (or maglev) trains. These don't have wheels but instead float above special rails enabling them to run at speeds of up to 370 miles per hour. A new generation of drones that are large enough to carry passengers will also make it possible to fly right into city centers, landing on top of offices and apartment blocks.

Green heights

Our towns and cities need to become greener, too. New technologies mean it is possible to grow plants up the sides of buildings in so-called vertical gardens, which take harmful CO_2 out of the air and replace it with oxygen. Soon we might see the first vertical farms, which will also produce food for growing populations.

Building the future

The previous chapters have shown just how much the structures we build have evolved over the last few thousand years, and now it's up to you. What would you like to see in the future—and how would you build it?

Index

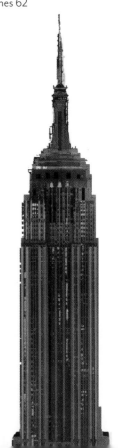